Final Deployment

poems by

Ann Quinn

Finishing Line Press
Georgetown, Kentucky

Final Deployment

*In memory of my mother, Jane
and for my father, Jim*

Copyright © 2018 by Ann Quinn
ISBN 978-1-63534-432-5 First Edition
All rights reserved under International and Pan-American Copyright Conventions. No part of this book may be reproduced in any manner whatsoever without written permission from the publisher, except in the case of brief quotations embodied in critical articles and reviews.

ACKNOWLEDGMENTS

Thank you to the editors of the journals in which the following poems first appeared (sometimes in earlier versions):

Beechwood Review: "Ma" (Pushcart nominee)
Potomac Review: "Watercolor"
Vietnam War Poetry: "Navy Junior" and "Three Years after My Father's Final Deployment to the Gulf of Tonkin"
Anima: "All-Soul's Eve" and "Mothers Day, 2014" (from "Elegy for my Mother")
Haibun Today: "Early morning mind"
Dragonfly Journal: "So much"
Urbanite: "Stories from my mantel"
Bethesda Literary Arts Festival Poetry Competition: "Three Years after My Father's Final Deployment to the Gulf of Tonkin" won 1st prize in the 2015 poetry competition, and was subsequently published on the website and in the Writer's Center blog.

Publisher: Leah Maines
Editor: Christen Kincaid
Cover Art: Jeanne Quinn, www.jeannequinnstudio.com;
        Photo by Matthew Weedman
Author Photo: Eric Sloan, www.windylanephotography.com
Cover Design: Elizabeth Maines McCleavy

Printed in the USA on acid-free paper.
Order online: www.finishinglinepress.com
        also available on amazon.com

Author inquiries and mail orders:
Finishing Line Press
P. O. Box 1626
Georgetown, Kentucky 40324
U. S. A.

Table of Contents

I.

Ma 1
At First 2
Early morning mind 3
Watercolor 4
83rd St. North Notebook 5
Navy Junior 6
Carrier Landing 8
Three years after my father's final deployment
    to the Gulf of Tonkin 9
Stories from my mantel 10

II.

Elegy for my mother 12
The Tragedy 17
Blind 19
A Safe Place 20
I take my mother to Johns Hopkins for a second opinion .. 23
So much 24
Payload 25
Systems Management 26
To a Catbird in May 28
The Great Wave off Kanagawa 29
All-Soul's Eve 30
Recitative 31

I.

Ma

> *In Japan, Ma is the essential space of nothingness—
> the empty, the void.*

I've been thinking about the in-between
places lately like the space between
words and the silence between notes
the summer between school years
the nights between days and how
essential the in-betweens are and what
I'm wondering is if death is the in-between
space or if life is

At First

Each child
and mother start from this:
scared treble of a voice
whispering the short refrain
I can't, I can't
two words forbidden,
unbidden

In this place you and I
begin,
you will carry my shadow
I so free till now
shackled to your soul

(what I believed I could not
for you I will)

Early morning mind

I wake at 2 a.m., lying on a couch in my sister's apartment in Boulder, my six year old daughter asleep on a mat beside me. Plagued by jet lag and early waking, but two a.m.? — I try all my usual tricks, listening to rain on my iPad, reciting rhyming poetry in my mind's ear, feeling for my pulse in each finger, but my mind will not let go. Finally, I risk waking Rose by turning on a soft light to find the volume of Chinese poetry I bought at a used book store yesterday. In "A Restless Night in Camp," Tu Fu advises: "It is useless to worry, / Wakeful while the long night goes." The blunt words from this distant world at last begin to quiet my mind.

> my thoughts
> as if in translation
> simplify, sleep

Watercolor

> *At home you will need something more ...*
> -*Welcome Aboard: A Service Manual for the Naval Officer's Wife*

I can no longer see it, but when I was a child there was always
a smiling face in this picture. A sailboat is pulled up to the dock.
A person kneels, elbows on the gunwale, speaking with the sailor.

Both are simple stock fill-ins of people, the inverted triangle
of a torso, the brown strokes of legs. It was their hats, I think,
that looked to me like eyebrows on a smiling face. There is no

mastery here, it was from my mother's first and last
watercolor class, years before my birth. But the colors
are pleasing, the light blue of the water, and the way each

horizontal brushstroke resembles a wave. The sky
a different shade of blue, with purples and grays, and white
spaces left for clouds, the hills on the far shore rounded, womanly.

Now I see, those are the San Diego hills—she must have
painted this in Coronado, newly married, following the directive
of optimistic busy-ness for the new wife:

*At home you will need something more than housework to keep
you occupied ... take a course in a language, sewing, weaving,
pottery making, bridge.* Of course!

She wasn't teaching, this tour was too short.
So she took a watercolor class on that cozy island
where my father rode to work on a scooter and was home

every evening. How I wish I could have lived there for a bit, but
my father's defection from Vietnam, but not the Navy, meant
no more ship duty for him, and we were sent East. Still,

I have this bright picture of the time before the war. I see
my mother's hand in the brushstrokes, her dark hair in the trunk
of the tree, her likeness in the birds vanishing into the California sky.

83rd St. North Notebook

Always the palm trees, the plane touching down.
But here it was old Florida, shaded by the huge live oak.
Right away we had to smell the gardenia, taste the kumquat.
We saw the street corner where Uncle Dave died, nineteen.
The appliances immortal, the furniture arranged in 1946.
Did they bring the smell of Illinois with them?
The St. Pete Times, the newspaper bags crocheted into doilies.
The Bible, the daily inspirational booklets, lifelong subscription.
A framed print Dave's last paycheck bought—a boy
      fishing among the palmettos.
Soft-skinned oranges, grapefruit like round bags of juice.
Being shown off to the neighbors—sometimes we had to read aloud.
Once I put a pretty bead in my ear and we went to the doctor.
Every other mishap my grandpa could fix me up.
"Sodey water" when I ate too much candy.
Splinters out with a big needle or a jackknife.
Puzzles, cards, buck-eyes from the farm.
Washtub I bathed in, till I was brave enough to shower.
Feeling of sharp Florida grass on my tender feet.
Taking the boat out of the shed, to the Bay, through the mangrove knees.
The pier, the huge brown pelicans like flying dinosaurs.
The muddy taste of just-caught sunfish, the spill of their guts.
Grandpa's temper at dinner, his meanness to grandma.
The unfairness of it a knot in my stomach.
Which remained clenched through the bedtime devotional readings.
The jiggly bed, the knick-knack shelf Grandma found
      in the chicken coop.
I caught a toad, felt its pee in my hands.
There was another shed full of dead things in formaldehyde.
Also rattles and fangs and discarded skins and bones.
With Grandma's Singer treadle, we sewed laundry bags from bits of cloth.
The only evidence of my mother was two framed photos.
I could never picture her living here.

Navy Junior
    Lemoore, California, 1967

1. Digging to China

Days we play indoors,
away from the heat and smog.

Evenings, I climb the jungle gym
my father put together

Like a big sturdy
Tinkertoy.

I dig in the backyard sand
with a spoon.

Digging to China
my mother says.

the grown-ups talk about
Indo-China
where the fathers are now.

I dig harder.

2. First Stitches

My beloved rocking horse
on springs, a bucking bronco.

Grandmother watching us
while mother joins father
in Japan, the carrier docked
for two weeks.

I rear back into a brick
garden wall.

The warm blood, grandmother
frantic, the ether,
the black stitches
painless.

3. Navy Junior
    Somewhere else, later

We moved every two years.
Our parents got good at buying houses.
We never lived on base.

Mother would find a church right away—
A place to belong. Usually
Presbyterian, though she grew up
Methodist. Father timed
the sermons—Presbyterians
know other Sunday demands.

But sometimes it was another denomination.

Presbyterians change two words
in the Lord's Prayer and leave out two more.
Not trespasses
but debts are forgiven.

I always inserted a moment of silence,
Forgive us our _____, so I wouldn't blurt
out the wrong word, revealing that
I was not one of them, whoever they were.

Carrier Landing

You have to learn to go against all
instinct, doing your utmost
to hook that cable while giving
your plane full throttle

Full speed ahead my dad would cry,
guiding his chatty female
family out the door; each of us grasping
at the strong cable of one another
even as we strove to take flight

Three years after my father's final deployment to the Gulf of Tonkin

In first grade we spent our free time drawing
on big sheets of soft urine-colored paper
the kind that would tear with no sound
like a piece of American cheese—
it would even muffle the sound of the pencil
darkening the page.
The other girls drew houses and people.
The boys and I drew planes
dropping bombs.

                    Were there people
on the ground? I just remember the difficulty
of drawing good planes. Because we were
drawing them from another pilot's point of view—
you saw the side of the plane, the cockpit,
and the bombs squeezing out the rear
like turds—but how to show the wings?
The wings were even worse than
the girls' task of drawing feet and noses.

Stories from my mantel

I polish the carved wooden elephant, its ears laid back and trunk raised as if danger is near, yet its eyes are placid, its four feet flat on the ground, so perhaps all is well after all. Thousands of U.S. servicemen must have purchased these hand-carved toys in the Philippines, on leave from the war in Vietnam, bringing a souvenir of an unhappy time to their children growing up so fast, asking every night, when will Daddy be home?

Another wooden toy, a crudely carved dachshund whose moving parts are held together with screws. Much older than the elephant, perhaps a hundred years old, American-made. He travelled from Illinois to Florida with my grandfather, who traded in his school principal post to run a Custard Castle at carnivals in the wondrous Florida of the late 1940's, a state covered with live oaks and Spanish moss, waters teeming with fish. After the first miserable winter in a beach house, his children feeding the gas meter with quarters, grandpa found a job teaching science at a junior high school. The dog looks wisely upon us all with his wry Buddha-like smile.

A clear glass lamp with a round handle like Aladdin's and a glass chimney that swells in the middle like a symmetrical light bulb. It looks like the light that Wee Willie Winkie carries in our old Mother Goose book. Called a "wick lamp", it burned with the newly discovered wonder-fuel, kerosene. It is intriguing, beautiful and terrifying, a memento from my grandmother's childhood. My great-grandparents, gentle and kind people, were farmers. I like to think of them walking through their quiet house like angels, carrying this light before them.

The newest artifact is a wooden crocodile, skillfully carved so that his whole body can flex as though made of rubber. My sister gave this to us when my son was very small. It's from a fair trade store, carved by a Central or South American paid a living wage. My sister is an artist too. She works with clay so her pieces are not appropriate toys for toddlers. Fired clay cannot be carved to simulate movement, nor can it be protected from shattering. She combines delicate porcelain pieces with light to make beautiful chandeliers that fill up a whole room. Now she has a baby boy of her own and so is learning about flexibility…

II.

Elegy for my mother

1. October 11, 1970

I am in my first grade
classroom in Lexington Park
Maryland. The teacher
has made a space capsule
from a card table and blanket.
Inside are two children picked
to be astronauts, a boy
and a girl named Christa Flynn,
pretty and blonde like her four
sisters. This year her father
will die in a training flight.

Today I am jealous that she
was chosen, not me
so she gets to hide in that
cramped dark space for as long
as she can bear it (pretending
to go to the moon). The real
astronauts who landed
on the moon when we were four
were once at test pilot school
like our fathers.

Three days a week I go
to swim team at the base
and when we drive through the gate
a man in uniform salutes
my mother
when she shows him
her officer's wife I.D.
and the kids in the carpool
crane their necks

to see the sign that tells
how many were injured
and how many have died
this year—
new numbers are exciting.

2. Palliative Care

It was to be a good death, a clean death, a loving death.
Hospice came every week and you learned all about the nurse's
bariatric surgery
because you weren't dying yet

and then suddenly you were.

At first there was to be no death at all
You would beat cancer the way people of faith
do, even when the doctors say there is no hope

prayer would find a way

But then the pain came, and the morphine—
blessed relief, for a time
skilled nurses on call

this would be fine.

The arrangements were already made, the funeral
pre-paid, the ashes to go
to separate cemeteries:

half with your parents and brother in Florida
in the Methodist cemetery
shaded with live oaks

the rest with your second husband's first wife
awaiting his demise in a soulless expanse
of tasteful markers and manicured lawns

to show your everlasting love.

Your daughters spent days with you in the death room
so there was much joy and singing and tears
the Christian folksongs unearthed—

the nurse said this would be a rich time

and it was but the death was fast coming
and not so clean after all because
when the organs break down

one cannot slip quietly into a good night.

So many pills to swallow when you can't even
keep down a bit of oatmeal or the good broth
your daughters made you, one here all the way from
Colorado with your grandson,

you'd worried about him but sent lots of prayers
just two years old with no father and you
want to let go into the loving arms of your

father and your mother and Jesus and grandmother

but it's so hard, the body just won't let go
and sometimes you see them and hold out your
arms to the light and people in the room are

beginning to talk about you as if you aren't there

but you are
only you can't make any sound
with your voice and it frustrates
so you retreat to your death rattle,

the place the morphine takes you.

You want to let go and go to Jesus
but this Earth holds you
so tightly, there is so much more to do,
it's all a mistake, you weren't supposed to die now

even though it's fine to die, soon, just not now.

Finally your eldest daughter says goodbye,
I love you, it's ok to go and the nurses say
it's ok to go and your first husband said it was ok to go

he came your last good morning—love recalled.

Your second husband hasn't come for days,
before that came only with his middle daughter you've tried
    so hard to love
he just couldn't stand to see you die
he was supposed to die first, a heart attack

you did your best but you can't hold on any longer—

3. Mother's Day, 2014

Here is lilac's
cloying thunder,
inescapable scent.

Maple wings clutter the sky
pilots parachuting
from doomed planes.

Oak catkins whirl down,
light bombs lathering the lawn
where violets watch

while lesser celandine, mocking,
invades
with bright heart-shaped leaf.

Daffodils already
shrouded in green.
Tulips beginning to fail,

their soft petals
opening helplessly
into poppies, then oblivion

or transfiguration.

The Tragedy

In Picasso's painting, the family stands huddled,
like oaks in a November storm.
The boy looks as old as his parents,
only half their height. He resembles

the young oak which holds its dead leaves
after the others have laid bare their branches
so that it looks at once both old and wizened
and young and naïve, that we could be fooled
by its cloak of wrinkled leaves
into believing winter not here.

He gestures to his parents
as if showing an idea, one
that would remove them from this desolate shore
and out of their ragged clothes,
and isn't it the duty of the young
to shake us from our despair

or our complacency, as when
Aylan Kurdi, age three,
washed ashore, face down in his velcro sneakers
to show us that within the great human
tides are humans—

that behind every act
of violence are the stories
and is that why my father taped
Aylan's last picture to the wall

beside the old photos of my sister and me
as children, and the newer photos
of our children, Aylan's age and so like him,
as penance for the bombs dropped in Vietnam,
(the awards for that hang there too)

* * *

My pilot father so close then to his childhood,
still believing comic book tales that the good guys will win
and those who can fly deserve to run the world
but now that certainty is gone

leaves released
yes, it is winter.

Blind

A man taps his way through the Metro station
into corners and out again,
the walls and railings guides
in this vast space. Watching him
find the escalator and ride
down to the platform, I wonder
Should I offer help?
but my children distract me
and he disappears. That night's

dream: Driving alone
on a dark road with no headlights
at full speed, using the curb
and traffic sounds as guides
and only a little frightened.
Then the sounds vanish.
I accept my coming death
with resignation.
Until a hand
touches my shoulder
and I wake

now I am afraid.

A Safe Place

I wake from a dark full sleep
and a poem rolls into my head
so I roll out of bed to grab it onto
a scrap of envelope and I'm in
such a good mood from the sleep
and the poem that I read Zagajewski
instead of the Times online while
I eat my turnip shallot spinach egg
concoction then I walk my daughter
to school and put away laundry—
it's what I always do but today
I just get right to it and then I go
to yoga and as I begin the
errands I've been avoiding (coffee,
cat litter, contact lens polishing)
I see four vultures on my street
and I'm happy because I've been
disturbed lately by the time and
energy I've put into this body and
I know I'll have to leave it behind one
day so it gives me comfort that
some creature will get some good
out of it though probably not
vultures unless I die in Tibet
and then I do my errands and the poems
will not stop coming and I'm even singing
along to *Bolero* which I normally don't care for
and I check the tires and do a car wash
thinking my kids need to experience this
while they're still kids safe in the car
with mom because it really is spooky
the noise and the menacing rollers
and then at the pet store I see two
women I know, friends or partners, I'm
not sure which and I tell one I like her

hair style (she usually wears a cap) and
she looks more pleased than I've ever
seen her and tells me it took five minutes
to style which would be really long
for me but her friend has a completely
new hair style and color every time
I see her so I'm guessing by five minutes
she means short and when she moves away I'm
reminded of the vultures' ungainliness
on land and I wonder what injury
or disease robbed her of two-legged
grace and I hope she has something
in her life that lets her soar and that's
not illicit and then later she shows up
at the writing group I lead and I read a poem
called "December" by Zagajewski
and invite people to begin writing with
his line *What you await is just now
being born* and she writes about her
happiness that she is about to move
into an apartment complex for seniors
and the disabled and for the first time
in her entire life will have a safe home

Here is what I write:
While it gestates, life must hide.
For safety—in the seed, in the bud.
Tightly closed, protected.
And still, of what is born,
so much is lost, dies. Think
of the maple wings, each
so perfectly constructed,
like twin virgin goddesses,
joined at the hip, so full of
life and promise, holding

not one but two maple trees
in each whirling self. Then imagine
if every wing in the fecund storm
of sufi dancing seeds in May
sprouted two saplings. And then if
all these saplings were allowed
to grow. Multiply this spectacle
by all of earth's species—no,
death must happen: it is birth's twin
and soul-mate. Even the Jains, who cover
their mouths with cloth to spare the
insects who might stray there,
hold within their bodies a universe
of life and death. My daughter
told me yesterday that she had saved
a fly's life. A friend had stepped on it
and instead of finishing it off, Rose
cradled it onto a safe leaf. She, at ten,
has not heard of *putting it out of its
misery* and after all how do we know
what misery is for another? All we know
is our own craving for safety,
a barrier between us and the vultures.

I take my mother to Johns Hopkins for a second opinion

Four to six months
without the drugs,

eight to twelve
with.

And now she is joyful
and strong.

No more
of that induced sickness,

just her and
the cancer.

We visit the statue
of Jesus

and take
a picture.

His arms outstretched.
Ours intertwined.

So much

Afterward going through your checkbook
in the last month custom make-up, a new crown
no plans to die soon.
But then, so much joy, so much light
we ended with singing, poetry,
the nurses disapproving:
this is not how you die.
One nurse, though,
Blessing. That was her name.
She sang to you at night,
songs from her country.
So much love.
Then the stoking breath, the vomiting.
You couldn't die with me there, so I wasn't.

Let me remember the light in your face.
Seen then, as now, through this scrim of tears.

Payload

After dinner, we're sitting in front of the family
portrait montage on the wall
by the kitchen, photos of five generations
back to our great-grandmothers, their hair
pulled softly back, their peaceful turn
of the century smiles, showing no teeth.
Somehow the great-grandfathers didn't make it
up there but our fathers did, in uniform—
Luke just seventeen and enlisted as a medic
on a troop carrier in the Pacific, my dad a pilot,
squatting in front of his jet in what he calls
"the only macho photo ever taken of me."
And he's remembering the only air show he
ever flew, how he volunteered because
the practices equalled ten hops, how
he got to fly the great ascent up through the
formation and he swings his arm and makes
the sound of a jet flying straight up into the air
saying, "That was to simulate the get-away
after an atomic payload drop" and then
there's a silence, a shift in the air, the ancestors
and the children on the wall still frozen,
their smiles fixed.

Systems Management

Pulling my daughter's shirt out of the dryer
where it tumbled for five minutes to get the wrinkles
out before hanging it on the pole stretched
across the laundry room, the shirt inside out,
washed this way

because my mother, when I did her laundry
shortly before she died,
told me that most of the wear in clothes comes
from the action of their washing and drying
so they will last longer if you turn them inside out,

though why I should care about extending
the life of this school uniform shirt
which she will certainly outgrow long before it wears out
is beyond me;

I wonder at her insistence that I let her hang
the shirt in her closet herself (after I've turned it
right side out) because she has a system, a certain
color for a certain day with the shirts lined up
in the correct order,

and I'm amazed that my little girl
has become someone who has a system at all,
let alone for weekday shirts,

—last night she told me
about her system for studying vocabulary words,
which involves writing each definition seven times,

and though I have created my own
systems for getting through life,

the beginning of her life
so completely defied any systems
attempted, no matter how many
parenting books we checked out of the library;

I marvel how
this expert disrupter of systems
already believes in them.

To a Catbird in May

Catbird, I write of change but
you sing of it from your wire
outbursting a raucous concatenation of spring.

For a moment you pause to listen
to the others then Shriek!
You're off again, flutters and snatches
of song, then a pause, then
Shriek! And if only I listen

No matter. You are like my small girl
who prattles in the back seat while
I battle with traffic. Or my mother-in-law
who chats on and on about the neighbors
while we rattle through the newspaper,
occasionally looking up to comment.

Silence implies vulnerability which
can be cured by vocalization. Sing on!
Spring is here, let the celebration linger.
Let the silent scribe your joy.

The Great Wave off Kanagawa

Picture Hokusai's famous print and consider
the thousands of hours he spent as an apprentice, then in his own
shop, sharpening pencils, grinding inks, cutting paper, refining
brushstrokes, developing the mastery to craft this image—

Imagine its history, its initial showing
in the Edo shop and its sale for the price of two
bowls of noodles, then decades later its voyage to Europe,
its effect on Debussy, Hergé, Degas...

Think of all the students who have studied this work
or glanced at it while turning through their texts,
and the myriad pages of scholarly insight in so many
languages, read left to right, right to left, top to bottom—

Count up all the money that has changed hands
over likenesses of this work on posters, mugs, keychains,
journals, pop art, t-shirts, silk scarves and all the other nothings
that can be made of a something we admire—

Now regard Hokusai's model, a version of which in the time
you've spent reading this poem has self-obliterated approximately
four billion eight hundred twelve times on all the world's
coastlines; smaller, yes, none tower over Mount Fuji, but each one
so perfect, in its motion harmony and violence, distilled—

Forget your worries about your place in this world.
We all, gentle lappers and giant rogues alike, will crash
one day and dissolve back into the same great ocean.

All-Soul's Eve
Deus, in adiutorium meum intende

the beauty intensifies just before dusk—leaves become luminous
    a glow enters the eye, a plainsong
    message from the dying sun

clouds in every form
    frail shrouds to mighty steel-sided ships

and what you believed in, and what shone from you
    magnified right before the end
    numinous in the last long rays

all questions are unanswerable, so why not live the answer
    that is oneness, love

air the paradox, ungraspable
just as the hand closes around, the wind steals it

better to let it carry you

under it all, a deep stillness
the sky a fresco—a quotidian mystery

the moon, a broken wafer
    multiplied in countless chalices formed of the earth's vestments

Vespers—as it was, it will be, forever—for a moment I understand
then Angelus, and the shadows lengthen until they vanish
Compline—a long darkness, but now I can discern Venus

    stars beginning to pierce the veil
    and I know that they are numberless
    if only I could see—

Recitative

When she senses my presence on the porch
from her fringe of nest folded into the sagging soffit
where she mothers with all her being,
her cries accelerate and crescendo
until she discerns that she scolds just
the back of a head—no eyes or claws
invade her small home. Her chirps quiet
to a dull metronome, set at sixty beats
per minute, just enough to assert
her presence. Whether it is to her mate,
her brood, the world at large,
or specifically directed to my yellow hat
I really cannot say.

Notes on the poems:

Early morning mind quotes from Tu Fu. "XXIII, A Restless Night in Camp," trans. Rexroth, in *One Hundred Poems from the Chinese*. New York: New Directions Pub., 1971

Poems are not literal. But these poems are based on literal memories, and when my father read *Digging to China*, part 1 of **Navy Junior** he pointed out: "The jungle gym (we called it a climber) was actually put together by Jim Busey. Jane had gotten to know his wife Jean, probably at the church, and they became good friends. I deployed from Lemoore in January, 1967 and Jim Busey deployed several months later, so he probably put the gym together about February, 1967. In the summer he led a strike on Hanoi for which he received the Navy Cross (Navy's second highest decoration after the Congressional Medal of Honor). I remember Jean coming over and saying, *Jim came back from a strike with 150 holes in his airplane*, which was true. He later was promoted to 4-star admiral, became Vice Chief of Naval Operations, from there went to become Commander, U.S. Naval Forces, Europe/ Commander NATO Forces Southern Europe."

In **A Safe Place,** the Zagajewski poem cited is "December," found in *Without End: New and Selected Poems*. New York: Farrar, Straus and Giroux, 2003

Additional Acknowledgements

With gratitude for all my teachers: my writing groups; faculty and students at the Rainier Writing Workshop; Lia and undergrads at UMBC, where all this began; my friends and teachers from The Writers Center, and of course the greatest teachers of all: my family.

Ann Quinn is a poet and essayist, editor, teacher, mentor, mother, and classical clarinetist. Her work has been published in *Potomac Review, Little Patuxent Review, Beechwood Review, Haibun Today,* and *Snapdragon,* and is included in the anthology *Red Sky: Poetry on the Global Epidemic of Violence Against Women.* She is a Pushcart nominee and first place winner in the 2015 Bethesda Literary Arts Festival poetry contest. She conducts writing workshops and music camps, volunteers in schools and libraries, and plays in a symphony orchestra. She lives in Catonsville, Maryland with her family. Visit her at www.annquinn.net